A-MAZE-ING ARIZONA

rising moon

Text © 2002 by Rising Moon
Illustrations © 2002 by:
Larry Jones
Joe Marciniak
David Brooks
Joe Boddy
Beth Neely
Susan Banta
Virginia Roeder

www.risingmoonbooks.com

Composed in the United States of America

Printed in Selangor Darul Ehsan Malaysia February 2017

Edited by Rebekah Bereit
Designed by Rudy Ramos

FIRST IMPRESSION 2002
ISBN 13: 978-0-87358-809-6
ISBN 10: 0-87358-809-6

ROAD TRIP!

Tour the Grand Canyon state. Make sure you visit all of the towns and attractions along the way—and don't pass the same place twice!

GO WEST!

Help this pioneer ride off into the sunset.
Don't get too close to the edge of the windy path!

FUN IN THE SUN

Find a pathway through the sun's rays and try not to get scorched.
There's *cool* water waiting for you on the other side. Don't forget your sunscreen!

PUZZLING POTTERY

Can you find your way through the pottery design to the top of the pots?

SHOW DOWN

Guide the Sheriff to the OK Corral, but watch out for "Bad Bart!"

EIGHT-LEGGED DASH

Walk carefully through these tarantulas and try not to step on any of them. These hairy creatures cannot see very well — so make haste and you'll be okay!

8

ESCAPING BY A HARE

Hop through the desert to your burrow before coyote eats you for dinner!

STEP RIGHT UP!

Climb the ladders and scale the walls as you venture into the ruins of this Indian village from one end to the next. Don't pick up any ancient artifacts along the way!

Finish

Start

DON RANTZ
BETH NEELY '01

11

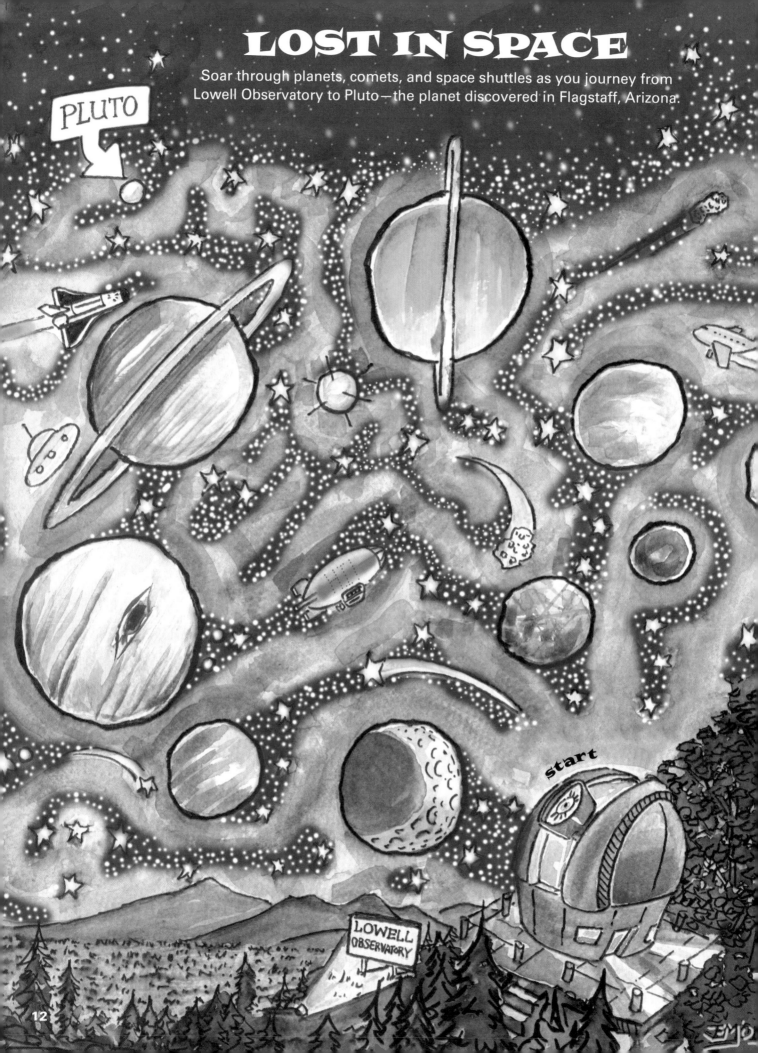

THE HAPPY HIKER

Help this hiker get out of the heat! Lead him from the sweltering desert to the cool mountain pines.

JEEP TOUR

Vroom! It's time for an off-road adventure. Drive through the
red rocks of Sedona for a picnic lunch beside the creek.

BELL ROCK

CAMP
GROUNDS

finish

PHOENIX RISING

This legendary bird rises out of its own ashes after
being consumed in fire. Clue: If you are on the right track,
you will wind through both wings before completing the maze!

Start   **Finish**

CRAZY FOR KOKOPELLI

Help the legendary flute player, Kokopelli, dance his way through this jumble of ancient rock art.

Start ▲

Finish ◀

FRESH POWDER ON THE PEAKS

Look out below! Lead these skiers to the bottom of Snowbowl; only one of them will make it to the finish line. Which one will it be?

FINISH!

PEEK-A-BOO!

Hidden inside a giant Saguaro is this tiny Elf Owl's nest.
Can you help him find his way back home?

SLIDE ROCK

Ride the rapids downstream to the apple orchard, but be careful of rocks in your path.

TREASURE HUNT

Have you heard of Lost Dutchman mine? It is said that there's gold inside.
Help this man find the treasure—maybe he'll share it with you!

Start

LOST DUTCHMAN MINE

QUICK SAND

Finish

DINO DIG!

Don't step on any dinosaur bones as you wind through
this archaeological site to reach your tent.

START

Finish

HOT! HOT! HOT!

Can you work your way from the bottom of the Chile Peppers to the top of the vine?

Finish

Start

24

DUST DEVIL

The sun and the wind can stir up a dust devil at any time. Can you help this bird fly safely through the dusty swirls to get to his friend on the other side?

LONDON BRIDGE

This boy's hat has blown off of his head into the water. Start at the top of the London Bridge and find your way through the bricks to retrieve it for him.

SNAKE, RATTLE, AND ROLL

Uh-oh! How did you end up in a place like this? You better s-s-sneak
your way to safety by following the connected diamond path, S-silly!

Finish

Start

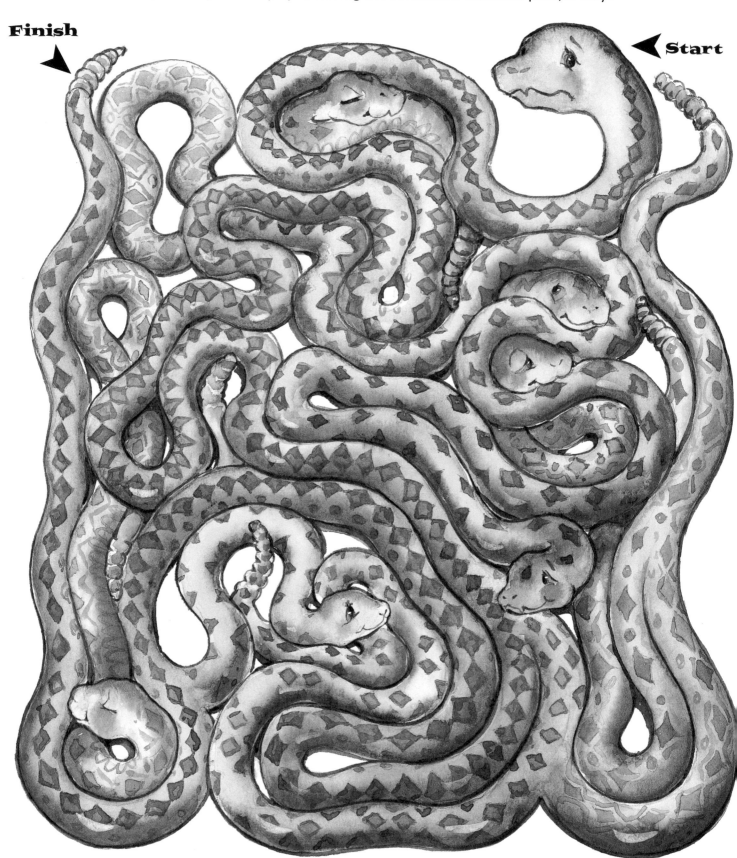

28

SADDLE UP, PARTNER!

Find the correct path that leads to Phantom Ranch.
Watch out for scorpions and dead-end trails.

DEAD END

DEAD END

PHANTOM RANCH

JEM '01

BEWARE OF BATS!

Grab your lanterns and your hiking boots! Explore Kartchner Caverns and all of its rooms without running into any bats.

THAT'S NUTTY!

Sandy the Squirrel knew her nuts would be safe in the Petrified Forest, but now she can't find them! Can you help her?

CHOO! CHOO!

Can you find a safe route for this steam engine to return to the station?
Be careful of bandits, rock slides, and fallen bridges.

CREEPY CRAWLY

Find your way through the scorpion lair without getting stung.

Start

Finish

GOT WATER?

Only one of these thirsty javelinas knows his way to the watering hole. Do you know which one it is?

37

CHECK, PLEASE!

Weave your way through the El Tovar Dining Room
and serve the hungry couple at table 14
their food before it gets cold.

BAH, BAH LOST SHEEP

Help these lost Big-horn sheep find their mother on the other side of Hoover Dam.
Don't fall in the water!

GIVE ME A BRAKE!

Wind your way through the steep hills of Jerome to the bottom of Cleopatra Hill.
Be sure to say "hello" to any friendly people you pass along the way!

BALL AND CHAIN

Help this inmate find his way out of the Yuma prison.
Be careful not to get caught by the guards!

SEE YOU LATER, NAVIGATOR!

Guide this houseboat, fishing boat, and jet ski safely to Wahweep Marina in Lake Powell, part of the Glen Canyon Natural Recreation Area.

42

WAHWEEP
MARINA

Loco for Lizards

Gila Monster's are known for their bite—they won't let go! Follow the yellow-back road from this lizard's head to its tail and don't dawdle.

DEWEY PUMPKIN PATCH

Nick, Sally, and Jake all want to find that perfect pumpkin. Guide them along the vines and show them the way. Who will be the first to get there?

ANSWERS

Page 1–Road Trip!

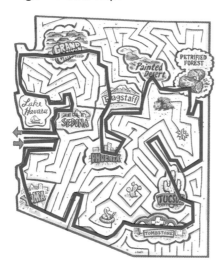

Page 5–Fun in the Sun

Page 2/3–Happy Trails!

Page 4–Go West!

Page 6–Puzzling Pottery

Page 7–Show Down

Page 11–Step Right Up!

Page 8/9–Eight-Legged Dash

Page 10–Escaping By A Hare

Page 12–Lost In Space

Page 13–The Happy Hiker

Page 17–Crazy For Kokopelli

Page 14/15–Jeep Tour

Page 16–Phoenix Rising

Page 18–Fresh Powder On The Peaks

Page 19–Peek-A-Boo!

Page 21–Treasure Hunt

Page 20–Slide Rock

Page 24–Hot! Hot! Hot!

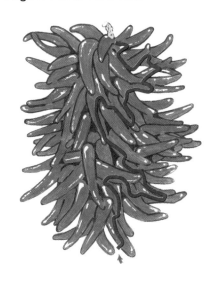

Page 22/23–Dino Dig!

Page 25–Dust Devil

Page 29–Saddle Up Partner

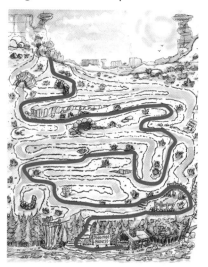

Page 26/27–London Bridge

Page 28–Snake, Rattle, and Roll

Page 30–Beware of Bats!

Page 31–That's Nutty!

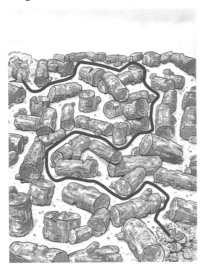

Page 34–Desert View Watch Tower

Page 32–Choo! Choo!

Page 35–Got Water?

Page 33–Creepy Crawly

Page 36/37–Tee Time

Page 38–Check, Please!

Page 40–Give Me A Brake!

Page 39–Bah, Bah Lost Sheep

Page 41–Ball and Chain

Page 42/43–See You Later, Navigator!

Page 44–Gila Monster

Page 45–Dewey Pumpkin Patch